MAY 10 2016

DANGEROUS DRUGS

E-CIGARETTES THE RISKS OF ADDICTIVE NICOTINE AND TOXIC CHEMICALS

ELISSA BASS

Cavendish Square
New York

S

Published in 2016 by Cavendish Square Publishing, LLC
243 5th Avenue, Suite 136, New York, NY 10016

Library of Congress Cataloging-in-Publication Data

Bass, Elissa, author.
E-cigarettes: the risks of addictive nicotine and toxic chemicals / Elissa Bass.
pages cm. — (Dangerous drugs)
Includes bibliographical references and index.
ISBN 978-1-50260-564-1 (hardcover) ISBN 978-1-50260-565-8 (ebook)
1. Electronic cigarettes—Juvenile literature. 2. Nicotine addiction—Juvenile literature.
3. Smoking—Juvenile literature. I. Title. II. Title: Electronic cigarettes.

TS2260.B37 2016
616.86'5—dc23

2015008940

Editorial Director: David McNamara
Editor: Fletcher Doyle
Copy Editor: Rebecca Rohan
Art Director: Jeff Talbot
Designer: Stephanie Flecha
Senior Production Manager: Jennifer Ryder-Talbot
Production Editor: Renni Johnson
Photo Research: J8 Media

The photographs in this book are used by permission and through the courtesy of: Librakv/Shutterstock.com, cover, 1; Headlinephoto/Splash News/Newscom, 6; PhotoQuest/Archive Photos/Getty Images, 7; USPTO, 10; Frederic J. Brown/AFP/Getty Images, 13; Max Faulkner/Fort Worth StarTelegram/MCT/Getty Images, 16; Elaine Thompson/AP Images, 19; BSIP/UIG/Getty Images/21; Jean Catluffe/Pacific Coast News/Newscom, 22; Frank Franklin II/AP Images, 25; SIPA/AP Images, 28; Lynne Gilbert/Moment Mobile/Getty Images, 31; Andrew Burton/Getty Images, 33; In Tune/Shutterstock.com, 37; Dan Henry/Chattanooga Times Free Press/AP Images, 39; Timothy Fadek/Bloomberg/Getty Images, 42; CDC, 44; Resound Marketing/AP Images, 45; Nicolas McComber/E+/Getty Images, 47; Joshya/Shutterstock.com, 50; Hal Bergman Photography/Getty Images, 52; Image Point Fr/Shutterstock.com, 55; STR/AFP/Getty Images, 56.

Printed in the United States of America

Contents

CHAPTER ONE

The History of Electronic Cigarettes

IN 2010, ACTRESS KATHERINE HEIGL WAS asked by talk-show host David Letterman about her smoking habit on *The Late Show*. Heigl admitted she started smoking when she was twenty-five, that it was a dumb habit to have picked up, and that she had tried many times to quit and failed each time. She had tried everything, she said, from the **nicotine** patch to the prescription drug **Chantix**.

Then, pulling an electronic cigarette out from under her leg, she said she had recently switched to electronic cigarettes, and she took in a big inhale. She took it apart, explaining the battery, the nicotine well, and how she is not breathing out smoke, but rather water **vapor**. She then handed the device to Letterman, who took a puff.

Actress Katherine Heigl advocates smoking electronic cigarettes over tobacco ones: "I'm totally addicted to the device."

"This is remarkable," exclaimed Letterman, who was a cigar aficionado prior to having a heart attack in 1999. "They have cigar-flavored ones," Heigl replied. "Is there a chance you can become addicted to the device?" Letterman asks. "Oh, yeah," she answers. "I'm totally addicted to the device."

For as long as there have been civilizations, there has been **tobacco**. It's been grown, harvested, turned into **cigarettes**, and sold for profit. America's first European settlers, in Jamestown, Virginia, grew and sold tobacco beginning in 1612. Tobacco was a cornerstone of the new American economy from the start.

During the 1800s, in large part due to the Civil War, cigarette smoking became an everyday habit for millions. Tobacco was given with rations to soldiers of both the North and the South. Advances in technology that allowed the mass production of cigarettes led to an explosion in the industry through the late 1800s and well into the 1900s. Philip Morris introduced its Marlboro brand in 1902.

By the end of World War II, cigarette smoking was widely accepted in all levels of society, and even women were openly smoking in public. Three hundred billion cigarettes a year were being produced, and the companies were making massive profits around the globe. Six main American cigarette companies—Philip Morris, R.J. Reynolds, American Brands, Lorillard, Brown & Williamson, and Liggett & Myers (now called the Brooke Group)—manufactured more than three

Smoking became a sign of sophistication for women in the 1920s.

Selling E-Cigarettes

The most popular claims in the marketing of e-cigarettes are:

- They are healthier than cigarettes.
- They are cheaper than cigarettes.
- They are cleaner than cigarettes.
- They can be smoked anywhere.
- They can be used to circumvent smoke-free policies.
- They do not produce secondhand smoke.
- They are modern.

Media coverage of e-cigarettes mirrors the advertising. A thematic analysis of newspaper and online media coverage about e-cigarettes in the United Kingdom and Scotland from July 2007 to June 2012 found five themes: healthier choice, circumventing smoke-free restrictions, celebrity use, price, and risk and uncertainty. Coverage often included anecdotes about having tried nicotine replacement therapies (NRTs), failing to quit, and then trying the e-cigarette (such as the celebrity endorsement by Heigl on Letterman's talk show), implying that e-cigarettes are a more effective form of NRT.

Traditional cigarettes can't be marketed on television. However, e-cigarettes have yet to fall under that ban.

hundred different brands of cigarettes. Collectively, the tobacco and cigarette manufacturers were making billions of dollars annually.

But in the 1950s and 1960s, scientific research began to show that cigarettes could be quite bad for your health. Tobacco smoke was linked to **lung cancer**, emphysema, and heart disease. In 1964, the **Surgeon General** of the United States issued a report that changed the course of the tobacco and cigarette industries, called *Smoking and Health: Report of the Advisory Committee to the Surgeon General*. Politicians began to enact laws that limited the use of cigarettes in public places, warnings were required to be attached to every pack, and cigarette advertising on television was banned.

The health of the cigarette industry suddenly wasn't looking as robust.

Coincidentally, in 1963, a man named Herbert A. Gilbert applied for a patent for the first electronic cigarette. Gilbert's device heated a nicotine solution and produced a water vapor. His patent, which was awarded in 1965, describes the device as a "smokeless nontobacco cigarette and has for an object to provide a safe and harmless means for and method of smoking by replacing burning tobacco and paper with heated, moist, flavored air; or by inhaling warm medication into the lungs in case of a respiratory ailment under direction of a physician."

Gilbert listed the advantages of his invention over traditional tobacco cigarettes in his patent application (note letter *d*, which states a medicinal value as well):

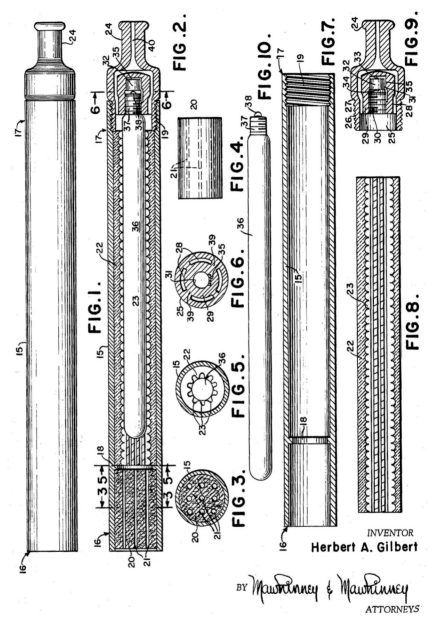

These drawings of an electronic cigarette were included in Herbert Gilbert's 1965 application to patent his invention.

(a) There is no open flame or fire, and fire hazard is therefore eliminated.

(b) Nothing is consumed, so that there is no smoke, ashes or dirt.

(c) Since the air that enters the lungs of the user comes into contact with only inert materials, there is nothing of an injurious nature being placed into the respiratory system of the user.

(d) Heated medication for respiratory ailments may be induced into the lungs of a user of this invention should a physician feel the same desirable.

(e) Persons who wish to smoke but have been advised against such a practice by their doctor may use this invention to maintain the satisfaction of smoking without any of its disadvantages.

(f) By changing the liquid employed to moisten the cartridge, a variety of tastes may be imparted to the warm, moist air that serves to duplicate the smoking sensation.

(g) The size and shape of the device according to this invention may approximate the size and shape of a cigarette; therefore its use will not call undue attention to the user. A white coloration of the basic tube and mouthpiece will further add to this illusion.

Before inventing the e-cigarette, Gilbert got a degree in business, joined the military and fought in Korea, and returned to work in his father's scrapyard in Western Pennsylvania. In an interview with the website www.ecigarettedirect.co.uk in 2013, Gilbert, now in his eighties, said he smoked two packs of cigarettes a day but saw that as a problem. "The problem, as I concluded, was that when you burned leaves and wood, even if you did it in your back yard, it yielded a result that no one wanted to take into their lungs."

He looked for a way to get the fire out of smoking and thought of the process of brewing tea. "Using logic I had to find a way to replace burning tobacco and paper with heated, moist, flavored air."

He said that he shopped his designs to chemical companies, pharmaceutical companies, and all kinds of manufacturers at the time, but he was unable to find someone willing to produce it. He felt that his idea was too far ahead of its time. His patent ran out, and he no longer has any of his electronic prototypes left at the scrapyard.

In fact, the e-cigarette's time didn't come for forty years. In 2003, a man in China, a heavy smoker himself who watched his father die of lung cancer, set out to create a "healthier" cigarette, using the same heated water vapor method first created by Gilbert.

Hon Lik was a pharmacist who was trying to get rid of his own pack-a-day smoking habit by using nicotine patches. "In the evenings I sometimes forgot to take off my nicotine

patch, which gave me nightmares all night," he said in an interview with Agence France-Presse, a global news agency.

Lik worked for a company called Golden Dragon Holdings. When the company began making his e-cigarettes, it changed its name to Ruyan, which means "like smoke."

In 2003, Hon Lik set out to create a "healthier" cigarette, using the heated water vapor method created forty years earlier.

In his patent application, Lik wrote, "Although it is commonly known that 'smoking is harmful to your health,' the number of smokers worldwide is up to 1 billion, and the number is increasing every year. According to the statistical data from the World Health Organization (WHO), about 4.9 million people die of smoking diseases each year. Although smoking may cause serious respiratory diseases and cancer, it remains extremely difficult for smokers to quit smoking completely."

He called his invention "an electronic atomization cigarette that functions as substitutes for quitting smoking and cigarette substitutes, and includes a shell, a mouthpiece, an air inlet provided in the external wall of the shell, an electronic circuit board, a normal pressure cavity, a sensor, a vapor-liquid separator, an atomizer, and a liquid-supply arranged sequentially within the shell."

The popularity of e-cigarettes has exploded since 2008, as studies show that awareness of the product has doubled among adults and adolescents in that time period. They have been widely heralded by manufacturers and in advertising as a completely harmless smoking alternative, but there is little research to back up that claim, and new research coming out is showing that there are hazards and concerns.

As e-cigarettes' popularity continues to grow, it is important to understand the full risk associated with their use for both the user and those exposed secondhand.

CHAPTER TWO

How E-Cigarettes Work

FOR THOUSANDS OF YEARS, HUMANS HAVE been filling pipes with tobacco, or filling small pieces of paper with tobacco, rolling them into narrow cylinders, lighting, and smoking them. It is estimated that around forty million Americans smoke cigarettes, fueling an industry that brings in $90 billion annually.

For a little more than ten years, humans have been mimicking the act of smoking tobacco cigarettes with a relatively new invention—the e-cigarette. The e-cigarette is charged by a battery, and does not use tobacco, but provides the same experience as traditional smoking for the user.

An electronic cigarette delivers a nicotine-infused aerosol to the user by heating a solution that is typically made up of **propylene glycol** or **glycerol** (glycerin), nicotine, and flavoring agents. An aerosol is a substance enclosed under

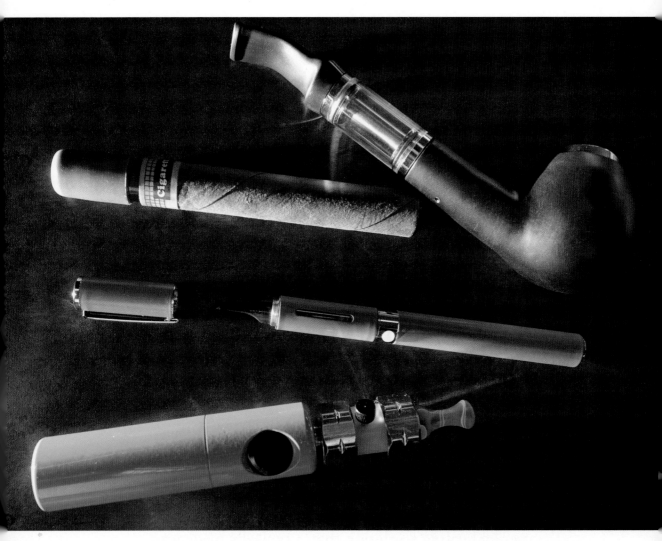

Electronic cigarettes are being manufactured to mimic every type of smoker's experience, and to deliver different amounts of nicotine.

pressure and able to be released as a fine spray. From China, where it was first manufactured in 2003, the electronic cigarette moved across Asia and Europe, arriving in the United States around 2007.

Electronic cigarettes are powered by a battery that heats the liquid solution. This creates the aerosol, which is called a vapor, which is inhaled by the user. This mimics the physical sensation of smoking. This process is called **vaping**. Sometimes people who smoke e-cigarettes refer to themselves as "vapers."

There are two basic types of electronic cigarettes. The "mini," also called the "cig-a-like," looks and feels like a traditional cigarette. It is small and lightweight. It comes in both disposable and rechargeable forms. According to e-cigarette sellers' websites, the mini makes the smoker's transition from traditional cigarettes to electronic cigarettes easier, they are lower cost, and they feel like a real cigarette in the hand. The downside of the mini is that it has a short battery life and may not satisfy a heavy smoker.

The next size up is the midsize e-cigarette, or "vape pen." These are typically the size of a cigar, and provide extended life and stronger vapor production. Usually, they are controlled with a push button, which is different from smoking a traditional cigarette. Websites that sell e-cigarettes recommend vape pens for heavy smokers.

The final size is the tank-style e-cigarette, which has a higher capacity battery and a much larger refillable cartridge to hold the nicotine liquid.

Repurposing E-Cigarettes

Electronic cigarette cartridges can be filled with substances other than nicotine, thus possibly serving as a new and potentially dangerous way to deliver other drugs. In some places, marijuana oil is being added to e-cigarette cartridges as a way to deliver a high to the user. The vapor produced by marijuana oil is mostly odorless, so people can inhale it in public without being detected.

School districts often ban smoking on school grounds. Now they are cracking down on possession of e-cigarettes because students are using them to vape marijuana. North Carolina, Washington, New Jersey, and Connecticut are among the states that are treating e-cigarettes as if they are drug paraphernalia. This can greatly increase the punishment for possessing one.

This concern is shared even in places where marijuana use is legal for people over the age of twenty-one, such as the state of Washington. Stores there are already selling the drug in prefilled cartridges. One administrator in Washington said students are taking a hit from e-cigarettes in classrooms when the teacher turns his or her back, and that they aren't inhaling tobacco. Students don't see this as harmful because the drug is legal.

"It's critical that our schools be free from negative influences," said Connecticut State Representative Devin Carney. "Countless studies show that electronic cigarette use among high school and even middle-school-aged kids is rapidly rising. Not to mention that many kids who would have never tried a traditional cigarette are experimenting with e-cigarettes—especially flavored ones. The bad habits brought on by them lead to the increased potential for addiction to nicotine-based products in the future."

Electronic cigarette catridges filled with marijuana oil don't emit the same telltale odor as a marijuana cigarette.

Disposables sell for anywhere from $7.99 to $10, and provide the nicotine equivalent of a pack of cigarettes. The reusable devices retail for $100 to $200. Refill cartridge packs vary in price depending on nicotine content (starting as low as $3), and liquid for do-it-yourself refills is sold, too. Each cartridge is good for several uses. Unlike regular cigarettes, which cannot be sold via mail in the United States under federal law, e-cigarettes, or e-cigs, can be shipped, so the online sales business for them is booming. In the United States alone, the e-cig market is worth $1.7 billion in sales. Some estimate that by 2023, e-cigarettes will outsell traditional cigarettes.

According to WebMD, no matter the type of e-cig, they all work the same basic way:

- The user inhales through a mouthpiece.

- Air flow triggers a sensor that switches on a small, battery-powered heater.

- The heater vaporizes liquid nicotine in a small cartridge (it also activates a light at the "lit" end of the e-cigarette). Users can opt for a cartridge without nicotine.

- The heater also vaporizes the propylene glycol (PEG) in the cartridge.

- The user gets a puff of hot gas that feels like tobacco smoke.

- On exhalation, there's a cloud of PEG vapor that looks like smoke. The vapor quickly dissipates.

- E-cigarettes contain no tobacco products; even the nicotine is synthetic.

When e-cigarettes were introduced to the Chinese market in 2003, they were being marketed as a smoking cessation device. With forty million smokers in the United States, that's a lot of people to sell to who might want to kick the habit. The WHO has already said that e-cigarettes cannot be marketed as a health device.

When they first came on the market, e-cigarettes were not banned from restaurants and other public places because they contain no tobacco and do not create smoke.

Actor Leonardo DiCaprio discreetly smokes an e-cigarette at the French Open tennis championship.

From the health perspective, marketers say e-cigarettes are good for people who want to be able to enjoy the act of smoking in the many smoke-free areas that have been legislated, including airports, restaurants, public parks, and work. Because the user exhales only vapor, and not smoke, e-cigarettes do not fall under smoking bans.

Marketers also claim that e-cigarettes supply the nicotine that smokers can be addicted to, without any of the dangerous or cancer-causing additives found in cigarettes, including the tobacco, the **tar**, or any of the six hundred other additives that manufacturers use.

Marketers also say that e-cigarettes are environmentally friendly because the vapors that are emitted dissipate quickly and because users discard their finished cartridges in the trash, rather than tossing their finished tobacco cigarette out a car window.

In addition, e-cigarettes seem to be particularly attractive to teens and twenty-somethings, people who were born long after cigarettes stopped being socially acceptable, and who have grown up in a world where smoking is illegal everywhere from airplanes to restaurants to public beaches.

The US Centers for Disease Control and Prevention (CDC) began collecting data on e-cigs in 2011. In the second year of data collection, among students in grades six to twelve, experimentation with e-cigarettes had doubled, to 6.8 percent from 3.3 percent. In 2011, 5 percent of high school students reported trying an e-cigarette, and in 2012 that figure had doubled.

To young people, e-cigs look like a way to smoke without smoking. And in part because of the number of young celebrities smoking e-cigs, including Leonardo DiCaprio, Britney Spears, and Lindsay Lohan, smoking is still "cool."

The industry's production of flavored e-cigarettes, ranging from cola to cake to fruits, candy, and alcohol, is also seen as an overture to entice young people to try them.

The WHO issued a report on e-cigarettes in the fall of 2014, calling e-cigarettes an "evolving frontier filled with promise and threat for tobacco control." The agency said regulations are needed to:

- Impede e-cigarette promotion to non-smokers and young people

- Minimize potential health risks to e-cigarette users and nonusers

- Prohibit unproven health claims about e-cigarettes

- Protect existing tobacco control efforts from commercial and other vested interests of the tobacco industry

Immediate action is needed to regulate two areas, WHO stated:

- Advertising: An appropriate government body must restrict e-cigarette advertising, promotion and sponsorship, to ensure that it does not target youth and non-smokers or people who do not currently use nicotine.

24

- Indoor use: Legal steps should be taken to end use of e-cigarettes indoors in public and workplaces. Evidence suggests that exhaled e-cigarette aerosol increases the background air level of some toxicants, nicotine, and particles.

The pervasiveness of electronic cigarettes in popular culture was solidified in 2014, when Oxford Dictionaries announced "vape" as the Word of the Year.

"Although there is a shortlist of strong contenders … it was vape that emerged victorious," Oxford explained in its blog announcement. "You are thirty times more likely

Vape shops, or vaporiums, carry an array of e-cigarette items.

to come across the word vape than you were two years ago, and usage has more than doubled in the past year."

Vape originated as an abbreviation of vapor or vaporize, according to Oxford. The word is also used to describe the actual device or "vape pen" used to inhale the liquids or "e-juice." Its definition was added in August 2014. Along with "vape" has come the word "vaporium," which is a place where people gather to smoke electronic cigarettes.

In the true spirit of entrepreneurship, vaporiums have been cropping up across the country. They also sell electronic cigarettes, associated equipment and paraphernalia, and vape liquids, or e-juice.

Vaporiums have joined hookah bars and medical marijuana smoking lounges as the newest venues for alternatives to traditional American smoking. In addition to having a place to hang out, vapers can customize the liquid to be vaporized, by flavor and amount of nicotine. They can buy specialized equipment to customize their e-cigarettes, and parts with which to build their own. Called APVs, or advanced personal vaporizers, these devices are being used for smoking marijuana and possibly other illegal drugs, officials fear.

CHAPTER THREE

Assessing Health Risks

SEVEN DECADES OF SCIENTIFIC RESEARCH have shown beyond all doubt that cigarette smoking is bad for your health. Since the early 1950s, researchers have linked tobacco smoke to lung cancer, emphysema, and heart disease.

In 1961, the American Cancer Society, the American Heart Association, the National Tuberculosis Association, and the American Public Health Association asked President John F. Kennedy to convene a national commission to study the effects of smoking. From 1962 to 1964 this commission met and reviewed more than seven thousand scientific articles. Surgeon General Luther L. Terry issued *Smoking and Health: Report of the Advisory Committee to the Surgeon General* on January 11, 1964.

The report held cigarette smoking responsible for a 70 percent increase in the mortality rate of smokers over non-smokers. The mortality rate is the proportion of deaths in a population. The report estimated that average smokers had a nine- to ten-fold risk of developing lung cancer compared to non-smokers. The report also named smoking as the most important cause of chronic bronchitis and pointed to a correlation between smoking and emphysema, and smoking and coronary heart disease. It noted that smoking during pregnancy reduced the average weight of newborns.

Based on the data, in 1965, Congress required all cigarette packages distributed in the United States to carry a health warning. In 1970, cigarette advertising on television and radio

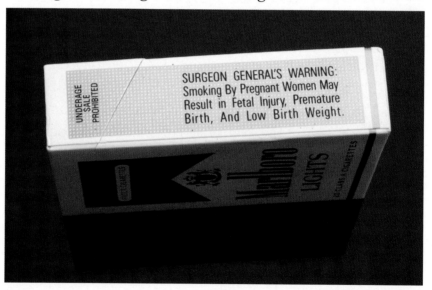

In 1965, Congress required that all cigarette packages distributed in the United States carry a health warning.

was banned. Studies since then cataloged the health risks for adults, adolescents, and pregnant women. In 1986, Surgeon General C. Everett Koop issued *The Health Consequences of Involuntary Smoking*, decisively portraying secondhand smoke as a very real health risk. Sustained exposure to secondhand smoke was equivalent to smoking about two cigarettes a day, and passive smoking contributed to more than fifty thousand deaths per year in the United States.

This finding provided an impetus for the banning of smoking in public places. In the span of one hundred years, smokers had gone from being widely accepted in society to becoming outsiders.

Then along came electronic cigarettes. Their popularity has exploded, as studies show that awareness of the product between 2008 and 2014 has doubled among adults and adolescents. In an annual government survey of forty-one thousand students, e-cigarettes are more popular among some teen groups than regular cigarettes. According to the survey, about 16 percent of tenth-graders had tried an e-cigarette in the past month, and 17 percent of high school seniors. Those totals are higher than the 7 percent of tenth-graders and 14 percent of twelfth-graders who had tried a regular cigarette.

Electronic cigarettes have been widely heralded by manufacturers and in advertising as a completely harmless smoking alternative, but there is little research to back up that claim, and new research is beginning to show that there are hazards and concerns.

Manufacturers and **proponents** of e-cigarettes say they are safe because they are not made like traditional tobacco cigarettes, which contain up to six hundred additives, many of which are **carcinogenic**. Proponents say because e-cigarette users are inhaling a vapor instead of tobacco smoke, and because e-cigarettes do not have the additives that tobacco cigarettes use, there are none of the traditional health risks involved.

Because e-cigarettes have existed on the mass market for only about a decade, the research into the health benefits or problems is in the early stages. So currently, both sides of the issue can lay claim that what they say is true.

The US Food and Drug Administration (FDA), which is currently reviewing proposed regulations on the electronic cigarette industry, says on its website that e-cigarettes have not been fully studied, so consumers currently don't know:

- The potential risks of e-cigarettes when used as intended

- How much nicotine or other potentially harmful chemicals are being inhaled during use

- Whether there are any benefits associated with using these products

Additionally, it is not known whether e-cigarettes may lead young people to try other tobacco products, including conventional cigarettes, which are known to cause disease and lead to premature death.

There are concerns about the way e-cigarettes are being marketed to youth, just as there were about cigarette advertising in the late 1960s. In 1970, President Richard Nixon signed a bill that banned cigarette ads on TV and radio. Use of cartoon characters to advertise cigarettes was banned in the late 1990s, and tobacco companies have been fined for targeting children with ads.

People are worried that similar tactics are being used now. Electronic cigarette advertising is using cartoons and sponsoring events popular with youth such as concerts and sporting events. A study published in June 2014 in the journal *Pediatrics* revealed that youth exposure to television advertisements for e-cigs increased by 256 percent from 2011 to 2013, exposing twenty-four million children to these advertisements.

Opponents of e-cigarettes say the flavored liquids are an enticement for teens to try the devices.

A blog posted in January 2013 by an e-cigarette manufacturer, titled *Why Do Celebrities Love e-Cigs?*, drew attention to celebrities popular among the young.

The blog post included the following: "It's not uncommon to find Robert Pattinson, Nikki Greene, Leonardo DiCaprio, Britney Spears, Paris Hilton, Jeremy Piven, and Katherine Heigl getting randomly photographed with their electronic cigarettes in use. This is proof that celebs are just like ordinary people, who want to overcome their use of tobacco cigarettes in favor of vapor. Here is a list of the reasons why stars have been quick to embrace using cigarette alternatives, and why they are working out to be so much better!"

The list included claims that e-cigarettes are better for the planet, healthier, not harmful to your complexion, convenient, and cooler.

But researchers are working hard to first determine and then catalog the ill effects of smoking e-cigarettes, and evidence is mounting that e-cigarettes are far from harmless. In fact, they can be as harmful as tobacco cigarettes, for different reasons.

One way is that higher-end models of e-cigs allow the user to adjust the voltage from the battery, which regulates the intensity of the heating element. As the solution gets hotter, it intensifies the effect of the nicotine hit.

The higher temperatures also can trigger a thermal breakdown of the solvents, converting them to some of the same dangerous chemicals found in cigarettes, such as formaldehyde and acetaldehyde, according to the Roswell

Park Cancer Institute in Buffalo, New York. In essence, by increasing the voltage to increase the nicotine "hit," e-cigarette smokers are creating some of the same issues that tobacco smokers face.

Users of higher-end models of e-cigarettes can increase the intensity of the heating element, making the nicotine hit stronger.

Other studies show that particles in the inhaled vapors can cause lung problems because of their size. Another study showed that after only a few minutes of use, e-cig smokers showed signs of airway constriction—as measured by several types of breathing tests—and of inflammation. And still another study showed that the inhalation of e-cigarette vapors could inhibit the effectiveness of certain antibiotics.

In addition, e-cigarettes are manufactured in China and shipped to the United States. In the wake of the device's explosive popularity, more factories have popped up in China, and quality control and regulation may not be up to American standards. According to a report in the *New York Times*, heavy metals, carcinogens, and other dangerous compounds, such as lead, tin, and zinc, have been found in some e-cigarettes.

The FDA collects so-called adverse event reports, which it defines as "an undesirable side effect or unexpected health or product quality problem that an individual believes was caused by the use of a tobacco product." Among the adverse events it has collected in connection with the use of e-cigarettes are hospitalization for illnesses and issues including:

- Pneumonia

- Congestive heart failure

- Disorientation

- Seizure

- Hypotension

- Other health problems

The agency goes on to say that "Whether e-cigarettes caused these reported adverse events is unknown. Some of the adverse events could be related to a pre-existing medical condition or to other causes that were not reported to the FDA."

The federal Department of Transportation started considering a ban on the use of electronic cigarettes on airplanes in 2011. The department was expected to enact the rule in 2015 despite facing some opposition to this decision.

"Anti-tobacco activists who disingenuously equate vapor and tobacco smoke may perversely convince smokers to reject far safer e-cigarette alternatives. Consumers should not be misled to believe e-cigarettes, which do not produce tobacco smoke and its many concentrated toxins, pose the same risks as smoked tobacco," writes Marc Scribner on CNN.com.

"To be sure, airlines should be free to ban e-cigarettes aboard their aircraft if they so choose. But just like the use of cell phones on planes (or a passenger's odoriferous perfume, for that matter), the risks posed by e-cigarettes do not justify federal regulation."

The Federal Aviation Administration wants passengers to be required to carry their e-cigarettes on board with them because of two instances in 2014 when electronic cigarettes that were packed in checked luggage caused fires.

WHAT'S IN THEM?

According to the Tobacco Vapor Electronic Cigarette Association, most electronic cigarettes contain the same ingredients, all of which are "generally recognized as safe (GRAS) by the Food and Drug Administration, have been in the food supply for generations, and as tested, contain no 'mystery' chemical of concern to the public or those who are tasked to regulate this market as laboratory research has been completed and by the FDA itself." Below are all the ingredients of an e-cigarette, and their amounts.

Propylene glycol—more than 50%

Glycerol—less than 30%

Nicotine—0 to 1.8%

Water—less than 10%

Alcohol (ethanol)—less than 1%

Coriander—less than 1%

Solanone—less than 1%

Citric acid—less than 1%

Benzyl alcohol—less than 1%

Orient tobacco absolute (flavor)—less than 1%

Pepper oil—less than 1%

Guaiacol—less than 1%

Menthol—less than 1%

Fragrant orchid element—less than 1%

What both sides do agree on is this: e-cigarettes have not existed long enough for anyone to know what the long-term effects might be, as they do with tobacco. Remember, cigarette smoking was widely accepted for nearly one hundred years in mainstream American society, and it was not until the 1950s, when the first long-term study results were released, that the true ramifications of tobacco smoking were understood. So the true health effects of e-cigarettes are likely years, possibly decades, away from being known.

CHAPTER FOUR

Social Problems, Hidden Dangers

"E-cigarettes are safe."

"It's not smoke, it's vapor."

"E-cigarettes are a great way to quit smoking."

THESE ARE ALL STATEMENTS THAT HAVE been uttered by manufacturers of electronic cigarettes at one time or another over the last ten years. And because the devices do not fall under any of the categories of smoking and/or tobacco-related products that the FDA regulates— cigarettes, cigarette tobacco, roll-your-own tobacco and smokeless tobacco—many consider the marketing, sale, and consumption of electronic cigarettes to be like the Wild, Wild West; that is, without rules or regulations.

According to its website, the FDA is proposing "extending its authority to cover additional products that meet the definition of a tobacco product under the proposed rule …

electronic cigarettes, cigars, pipe tobacco, certain dissolvables that are not 'smokeless tobacco,' gels, and waterpipe tobacco. Once the proposed rule becomes final, the FDA will be able to enact age restrictions and rigorous scientific review of new tobacco products and claims to reduce tobacco-related disease and death."

The most controversial aspect of the FDA's proposed regulations is that e-cigarettes would be classified as a new

Vaporiums have become hangouts for young adults. New rules could put small shops out of business.

tobacco product. This would require an enormously complex, rigorous, and expensive course of review prior to approval that would likely drive out of business the approximately 450 small e-cig manufacturers, leaving the industry in the hands of the large tobacco companies.

According to the FDA's estimates, the scientific investigations would take more than five thousand hours and cost more than $300,000. This type of review is commonly used to prove that very risky products, like drugs or pesticides, aren't harmful. But as proponents point out, it's not that e-cigs are safe, but that they are significantly safer than regular cigarettes.

Legislation was submitted in Congress in 2014 to try to tighten regulation on e-cigarettes; there were Federal Commerce Committee hearings, but the proposal died without action.

In March 2014, Congresswoman Elizabeth Esty of Connecticut introduced legislation called "Protecting Children from Electronic Cigarette Advertising Act of 2014" that would act "to prohibit the marketing of electronic cigarettes to children, and for other purposes."

The Act would have the Federal Trade Commission "prohibit the advertising, promoting, and marketing in commerce of electronic cigarettes to children as an unfair or deceptive act or practice, in order to protect the health of the youth of the United States."

The bill lays out the issues surrounding the lack of research findings about the health effects of electronic cigarette use.

Among these are the fact that the benefits or dangers of electronic cigarettes have not been fully studied; it's unclear how much nicotine or other potentially harmful chemicals are being inhaled during use; and that electronic cigarettes contain widely varying levels of nicotine, which impacts the cardiovascular system and can be lethal when delivered in high doses.

Further, there are concerns over the effect of e-cigarettes on children and adolescents. They are especially vulnerable to the adverse effects of nicotine and may have their brain development permanently harmed.

Twenty-six states regulate electronic cigarettes in some way. Minnesota and North Carolina were the first two states to tax e-cigarettes. The 2015 Connecticut legislature has a number of bills involving the regulation of e-cigarettes, including a bill that would ban them from school property.

What are the concerns associated with the use of electronic cigarettes? Let's look at them one by one.

Nicotine Is Addictive

Once introduced into the body, nicotine is absorbed into the bloodstream. When it reaches the brain through the blood, it causes the brain to release adrenaline, creating a "buzz" of pleasure and energy. Nicotine acts as a mood regulator, some people say it helps them think more clearly, and it also works as an appetite suppressant (which is why smokers who quit generally gain weight). There's even hotly debated research that suggests it may slow the onset of Alzheimer's disease.

Problems Arise with Popularity

In April 2014, the CDC reported an astronomical rise in the number of calls to poison control centers because of the use of electronic cigarettes by children.

In 2010, poison control centers across the nation averaged one call per month involving someone sickened by use of an e-cigarette. In 2014, the average was two hundred per month. Perhaps more concerning than even that dramatic increase is this: although e-cigs comprise less than 2 percent of all tobacco-related sales, they account for more than 40 percent of poison center calls. And more than half of those calls involved children younger than five years old.

Most of the calls involved what is called **acute nicotine toxicity**, which comes from direct exposure to the liquid nicotine in e-cigarettes. If the cylinder that holds the liquid is broken open, the liquid nicotine can be swallowed or its fumes inhaled. Even just exposure to the skin can cause illness.

Nicotine liquid flavors including cake, cola, and strawberry can attract young children.

The downside is that the "buzz" quickly fades and leaves you feeling tired and a little depressed. The human body is able to build up a high tolerance to nicotine, resulting in the need to smoke more and more cigarettes in order to get the nicotine's pleasurable effects and prevent withdrawal symptoms. This up and down cycle repeats over and over, leading to addiction, just like it works with narcotics.

Research suggests that children and teens may be especially sensitive to nicotine, making it easier for them to become addicted. The younger smokers are when they start, the more likely they are to become addicted. In fact, three out of four high school smokers will become adult smokers.

Gateway to Tobacco

Because e-cigarettes are marketed as "safer than smoking," research is showing that teens are turning to them in large numbers. In 2013, the CDC reported that the percentage of US middle- and high-school students who use electronic cigarettes more than doubled from 2011 to 2012. The data came from a survey of eighteen thousand teenagers.

In a press release, the CDC reported the results of the National Youth Tobacco Survey. It showed that the percentage of high school students that had used an e-cigarette rose from 4.7 percent in 2011 to 10.0 percent in 2012. In the same time period, high school students using e-cigarettes within the past 30 days rose from 1.5 percent to 2.8 percent. Use also doubled among middle school students. Altogether, in 2012, more than 1.78 million middle- and high-school students nationwide had tried e-cigarettes.

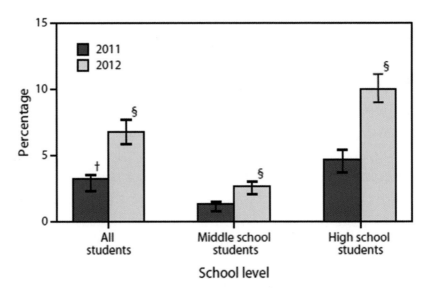

From 2011 to 2012, the percentage of middle and high school students who reported having used e-cigarettes increased.

The study also found that 76.3 percent of middle- and high-school students who used e-cigarettes within the past thirty days also smoked conventional cigarettes in the same period. In addition, one in five middle-school students who reported ever using e-cigarettes say they have never tried conventional cigarettes.

"About 90 percent of all smokers begin smoking as teenagers," said Dr. Tim McAfee, director of the CDC Office on Smoking and Health. "We must keep our youth from experimenting or using any tobacco product. These dramatic increases suggest that developing strategies to prevent marketing, sales, and use of e-cigarettes among youth is critical."

44

"The increased use of e-cigarettes by teens is deeply troubling," said CDC Director Dr. Tom Frieden. "Nicotine is a highly addictive drug. Many teens who start with e-cigarettes may be condemned to struggling with a lifelong addiction to nicotine and conventional cigarettes."

Accessible to Children

Because electronic cigarettes are still unregulated by the FDA, they are not universally subjected to any of the restrictions that tobacco cigarettes are, including the banning of their use in public places, the banning of television advertisements,

TV personality Jenny McCarthy advertises a brand of electronic cigarettes.

and the banning of their sale to anyone under eighteen years of age.

E-cigarette ads are regularly aired on television, including one featuring television personality Jenny McCarthy, who says, "It doesn't make my hair smell or my teeth turn yellow. And no going outside in the rain or freezing my butt off just to take a puff." Their use is not banned in bars, restaurants or public spaces. Electronic cigarettes can be purchased online and mailed to buyers, while tobacco cannot. And while the CDC reports that forty states have enacted laws prohibiting the sale of electronic nicotine delivery systems (ENDS), including e-cigarettes, to minors, ten states and the District of Columbia still permit such sales.

In 2013, New York City added e-cigarettes to its ban of smoking in workplaces, bars, restaurants, parks, beaches, and plazas. In late 2014, the state of New York banned the sale of liquid nicotine to minors under the age of eighteen and required that all liquid nicotine sold in the state come in child-resistant packaging. In 2015, New York Governor Andrew Cuomo asked the state legislature to ban the use of e-cigarettes in areas where tobacco products are already prohibited.

More than a dozen local governments including Concord City and Petaluma in California, and Lee, Lenox, Stockbridge, North Attleborough, Pittsfield, Somerset, and South Hadley in Massachusetts also have similar laws, but the majority of communities do not.

Many states are enacting laws that limit access to e-cigarettes to anyone under the age of eighteen.

While e-cigarette smokers make much of the fact that they are not inhaling or exhaling harmful smoke, as tobacco smokers do, studies examining exactly what is in e-cig vapors are beginning to show that "harmless" is not an appropriate description.

Results of a study released in early 2015 showed that the vapors can contain a high concentration of formaldehyde—a known carcinogen. Researchers found what they called masked formaldehyde in the liquid droplet particles in the aerosol. They called it "masked" because it was slightly different from the formaldehyde found in tobacco. Perhaps most concerning was the fact that the vapors' formaldehyde was in a form that could increase the likelihood it would get deposited in the lung. The concentration of the formaldehyde was five to fifteen times greater than what is found in tobacco smoke.

CHAPTER FIVE

Beating Nicotine Addiction

CIGARETTE SMOKING IS THE LEADING preventable cause of illness and death in the United States—more than four hundred thousand Americans die every year because of cigarette smoking. The fatal consequences of smoking are linked to the inhalation of tar and the hundreds of other chemical additives to cigarettes. Addiction to smoking cigarettes is caused by the inhalation of nicotine, which is contained in the tobacco.

It is the nicotine addiction that makes it difficult for people to quit smoking, thus making cigarette smoking a preventable cause of illness and death: if four hundred thousand people didn't smoke cigarettes, they would not die of diseases related to that act.

Electronic cigarettes have eliminated tobacco, a fact that marketers exploit in their advertising of the devices.

E-cigarettes don't create smoke. Instead, they create vapors because they superheat a liquid rather than burn a dried leaf.

But that liquid contains nicotine. E-cigarettes can continue—or start—an individual's addiction to nicotine. And nicotine is highly addictive.

Why do smokers get hooked on nicotine? Nicotine is a drug that mildly stimulates the central nervous system and accelerates neuron activity all through the brain. Neurons carry messages from parts of the body to the brain. Nicotine affects neurotransmitters such as dopamine, affecting memory, arousal, attention, mood, and feelings of pleasure. Neurotransmitters carry chemical signals from one neuron to receptors on another across a gap called a synapse. When drugs artificially increase the release of neurotransmitters, their effect

The Action of Nicotine

Synapse without Nicotine

Synapse with Nicotine

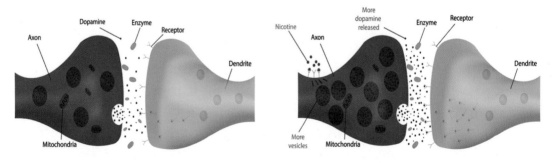

Nicotine increases the release of brain chemicals called neurotransmitters, which help regulate mood and behavior.

on the body increases. However, when drug use is repeated, the body produces fewer of its own neurotransmitters. So when the nicotine wears off, the body doesn't generate enough neurotransmitters that naturally regulate feelings of pleasure and the pleasure disappears. People then need to use the drug to feel normal again. This effect is called tolerance. People who want to repeat the high the drug produces must put more nicotine into the bloodstream. This is what creates the addiction.

The act of smoking also involves lots of behaviors that can become habits. Often, smokers have specific times of day they smoke or activities associated with smoking, ranging from drinking alcohol to talking on the phone. These habits can make quitting smoking more challenging.

E-cigarettes market themselves as providing that nicotine buzz and the physical satisfaction of smoking without the carcinogens and other illness-causing additives found in tobacco cigarettes. And while it is true that vapors are—at this point in the research—far less physically damaging to the human body than smoke, nicotine remains an addictive and dangerous drug.

The US Surgeon General has concluded that nicotine exposure during adolescence may have lasting adverse consequences for brain development.

Dr. Brian King, a senior scientific advisor in the CDC's Office on Smoking and Health, agrees with that opinion. He said an e-cigarette's aerosol "is not harmless water vapor; it

SIGNS OF NICOTINE ADDICTION

Nicotine produces physical and mood-altering effects in your brain that are temporarily pleasing. These effects make you want to use tobacco and lead to dependence. The Mayo Clinic, a nonprofit medical practice and medical research group based in Rochester, Minnesota, has created a list of signs that indicate you may be addicted to nicotine, which is found in both tobacco and e-cigarettes.

- You can't stop smoking. You've made one or more serious, but unsuccessful, attempts to stop.

- You experience withdrawal symptoms when you try to stop, including strong

A sign you're addicted to nicotine: you will stand outside in any weather to smoke a cigarette.

cravings, anxiety, irritability, restlessness, difficulty concentrating, depressed mood, frustration, anger, increased hunger, insomnia, constipation, or diarrhea.

- You keep smoking despite health problems. Even though you've developed problems with your lungs or your heart, you haven't been able to stop.

- You give up social or recreational activities in order to smoke. You may stop going to smoke-free restaurants or stop socializing with certain family members or friends because you can't smoke in these locations or situations.

can contain nicotine and other toxins. Exposure to nicotine can harm adolescent brain development and can be toxic to fetuses."

In addition, nicotine can cause pregnant women to deliver their babies prematurely, can contribute to the incidence of stillbirth, and can cause babies to be born underweight. Recent research suggests nicotine exposure may also prime the brain to become addicted to other substances.

Nicotine in its pure liquid form is highly toxic. Because e-cigarettes come with refillable nicotine cartridges, users can be exposed to potentially toxic levels of nicotine when refilling them.

So how can you quit nicotine? There are both over-the-counter (OTC) and prescription medications. The treatment in general is known as nicotine replacement therapy—it gives you nicotine without the other harmful chemicals in tobacco smoke or e-cigarette vapors. Nicotine replacement medications include patches, gum, lozenges, nasal sprays, and inhalers. Their use can help relieve difficult withdrawal symptoms and cravings.

According to the Mayo Clinic's website, here is how the different methods work:

Nicotine patch. The patch delivers nicotine through your skin and into your bloodstream. You wear a new patch each day. The treatment period usually lasts for eight weeks or longer.

Nicotine gum. This gum delivers nicotine to your blood through the lining of your mouth. It's available in a 2-milligram (mg) dose for regular smokers and a 4 mg dose for heavy smokers. Nicotine gum is often recommended to curb cravings. It allows nicotine to be gradually absorbed into your bloodstream. The goal is to reduce the amount and eliminate the need for the gum in about three months.

Nicotine lozenge. This lozenge dissolves in your mouth and, like nicotine gum, delivers nicotine through the lining of your mouth. The lozenges are available in a 2 mg dose for regular smokers and a 4 mg dose for heavy smokers.

54

Nicotine nasal spray. The nicotine in this product, sprayed directly into each nostril, is absorbed through your nasal membranes into your blood vessels. The nasal spray delivers nicotine a bit quicker than gum, lozenges, or the patch, but not as rapidly as smoking a cigarette. It's usually prescribed for three-month periods for up to six months. Side effects may include nasal irritation.

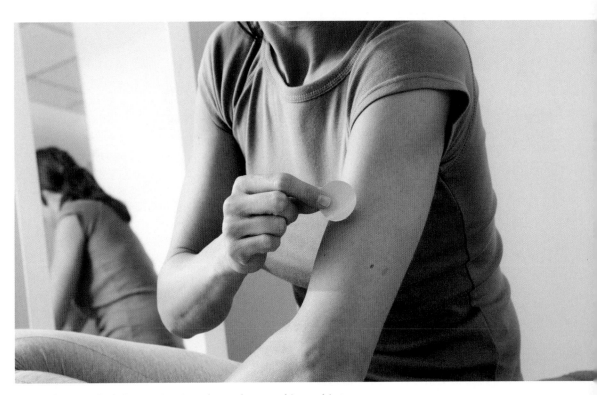

A nicotine patch delivers nicotine through your skin and into your bloodstream.

Nearly all the e-cigarettes in the US are made in China, where there is little to no factory oversight to ensure manufacturing standards.

Nicotine inhaler. This device is shaped something like a cigarette holder. You puff on it, and it delivers nicotine vapor into your mouth. You absorb the nicotine through the lining in your mouth, where it then enters your bloodstream. Common side effects are mouth or throat irritation and occasional coughing.

Prescription medication. The pharmaceutical company Pfizer Inc. invented Chantix, a nicotine-free prescription pill that is taken for twelve weeks (three months), along with support, to help someone quit smoking. More than ten million prescriptions have been written for it since it came on the market in 2006. Chantix works by connecting to the nicotine receptors in the brain, causing the dopamine to be released.

Among the side effects associated with the use of Chantix are changes in behavior, hostility, agitation, depressed mood, suicidal thoughts or actions, anxiety, panic, aggression, anger, mania, abnormal sensations, hallucinations, paranoia, or confusion. Some people have seizures during treatment with Chantix.

And while some people say that e-cigarettes can help smokers kick the habit, the FDA has determined that companies cannot call them nor market them as smoking cessation devices. Because they still deliver nicotine to the user, and because newer generation models allow users to increase the amount of nicotine delivered in each puff, there is a strong belief among healthcare providers that e-cigarettes

will ultimately do as much harm as tobacco cigarettes, just in a different way.

The liquid used in e-cigarette cartridges is manufactured primarily in China, and there is growing concern that the lack of regulatory oversight of the production processes in that country could lead to even more health concerns in the future. Testing of those cartridges shows a lack of consistency in ingredients, and sometimes the inclusion of dangerous materials, including metals.

GLOSSARY

acute nicotine toxicity A toxic effect produced by nicotine.

addiction The state of being enslaved to a habit or practice or to something that is psychologically or physically habit-forming, such as narcotics, to such an extent that stopping its use causes severe trauma.

carcinogenic Any substance or agent that has the potential to cause cancer.

Chantix The brand name for the prescription drug verenicline, which is prescribed to aid in the cessation of smoking.

cigarette A cylindrical roll of finely cut tobacco cured for smoking, usually wrapped in thin, white paper.

glycerol A colorless, odorless, syrupy, sweet liquid, used for sweetening and preserving food, and in the manufacture of cosmetics, perfumes, inks, and certain glues and cements.

lung cancer A cancer (malignancy) that originates in the lungs when normal lung cells become cancer cells, usually after a series of mutations, and begin to divide out of control.

nicotine A colorless, oily, water-soluble, highly toxic, liquid alkaloid, $C_{10}H_{14}N_2$, found in tobacco and valued as an insecticide.

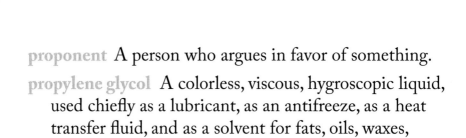

proponent A person who argues in favor of something.

propylene glycol A colorless, viscous, hygroscopic liquid, used chiefly as a lubricant, as an antifreeze, as a heat transfer fluid, and as a solvent for fats, oils, waxes, and resins.

Surgeon General The operational head of the US Public Health Service Commissioned Corps (PHSCC) and thus the leading federal spokesperson on matters of public health.

tar Any of various dark-colored viscid products obtained by the destructive distillation of certain organic substances, such as coal or wood.

tobacco Any of several plants belonging to the genus Nicotiana, of the nightshade family, especially one of those species, as N. tabacum, whose leaves are prepared for smoking or chewing or as snuff.

vaping To draw in and exhale the vapor from an e-cigarette or similar device.

vapor A visible exhalation, such as fog, mist, steam, smoke, or noxious gas, diffused through or suspended in the air; gaseous particles of drugs that can be inhaled as a therapeutic agent.

Find Out More

Books

Burgan, Michael. *Tobacco and Nicotine. Dangerous Drugs*. New York: Cavendish Square Publishing, 2014.

Fox, Georgia L. *The Archaeology of Smoking and Tobacco*. American Experience in Archaeological Perspective. Gainesville, FL: University Press of Florida, 2015.

Horsfield, Alan, and Elaine Horsfield. *Talking About the Dangers of Alcohol, Tobacco, and Caffeine*. Healthy Living. New York: Gareth Stevens, 2010.

Kuhar, Michael. *The Addicted Brain: Why We Abuse Drugs, Alcohol, and Nicotine*. Upper Saddle River, NJ: FT Press Science, 2011.

Laugesen, Dr. Murray. *Nicotine and Health*. New York: American Council on Science and Health, 2013.

US Centers for Disease Control and Prevention

www.cdc.gov/tobacco/basic_information/e-cigarettes/youth-intentions/index.htm

This site contains a tremendous amount of information about electronic cigarettes, adult and youth usage, health risks, reported health problems, regulations, state laws, and more.

US Food and Drug Administration

www.fda.gov/NewsEvents/PublicHealthFocus/ucm172906.htm

Information about the ongoing debate over the regulation of electronic cigarettes, studies, and about tobacco and nicotine.

WebMD

www.webmd.com/a-to-z-guides/electronic-cigarettes-topic-overview

Read unbiased coverage of the health issues surrounding the use of e-cigarettes, including concise explanations of how the devices work. Pages include an overview, a Q&A, and more. There is also good information about nicotine addiction and health issues related to tobacco usage.

Page numbers in **boldface** are illustrations. Entries in **boldface** are glossary terms.

About the Author

Elissa Bass is an award-winning journalist who has been a reporter and editor for both print and online publications for thirty years. Born and raised in western Massachusetts, she makes her home in Stonington, Connecticut, with her husband, their two children, and their rescued pit bull.